# 50 Ultimate Home Cooking Recipes

By: Kelly Johnson

# Table of Contents

- Classic Roast Chicken
- Beef Stroganoff
- Spaghetti Carbonara
- Chicken Parmesan
- Homemade Mac and Cheese
- Classic Meatloaf
- Garlic Butter Shrimp
- Baked Ziti
- Chicken Alfredo Pasta
- Slow Cooker Pot Roast
- Stuffed Bell Peppers
- Shepherd's Pie
- Chicken Tikka Masala
- French Onion Soup
- BBQ Pulled Pork
- Shrimp Scampi
- Homemade Pizza
- Chicken Fajitas
- Baked Salmon with Lemon
- Creamy Mushroom Risotto
- Classic Lasagna
- Beef Tacos
- Lemon Herb Roast Chicken
- Clam Chowder
- Crispy Fried Chicken
- Teriyaki Chicken
- Chicken and Dumplings
- Sweet and Sour Pork
- Homemade Chili
- Chicken Pot Pie
- Beef and Broccoli Stir-Fry
- Grilled Cheese and Tomato Soup
- Tuna Casserole
- Meatball Subs
- Pancakes from Scratch
- French Toast

- Shrimp Fried Rice
- Classic Caesar Salad with Chicken
- Homemade Burgers
- Beef Wellington
- Cajun Jambalaya
- Greek Moussaka
- Korean Bibimbap
- Vegetable Stir-Fry
- Slow Cooker Ribs
- Lobster Bisque
- Chicken Cordon Bleu
- Eggplant Parmesan
- Classic Beef Stew
- Apple Pie

## Classic Roast Chicken

### Ingredients:

- 1 whole chicken (about 4-5 lbs)
- 2 tbsp olive oil or melted butter
- 1 lemon, halved
- 4 garlic cloves, smashed
- 1 tbsp salt
- 1 tsp black pepper
- 1 tsp paprika (optional)
- 1 tsp dried thyme or rosemary
- 1 onion, quartered
- 2 carrots, cut into chunks
- 2 celery stalks, cut into chunks

### Instructions:

1. Preheat oven to 425°F (220°C).
2. Pat the chicken dry with paper towels.
3. Rub olive oil or melted butter all over the chicken.
4. Season inside and out with salt, pepper, paprika, and thyme.
5. Stuff the cavity with lemon halves, garlic, and some onion pieces.
6. Place chicken breast-side up in a roasting pan with remaining onions, carrots, and celery.
7. Roast for about 1 hour 15 minutes, or until internal temperature reaches 165°F (75°C).
8. Let rest for 15 minutes before carving.
9. Serve warm and enjoy!

**Beef Stroganoff**

**Ingredients:**

- 1 lb beef sirloin or tenderloin, sliced thinly
- 2 tbsp olive oil
- 1 small onion, chopped
- 2 cloves garlic, minced
- 1 cup beef broth
- 1 tbsp Worcestershire sauce
- 1 tbsp Dijon mustard
- 1 cup sour cream
- 2 tbsp flour
- Salt and pepper, to taste
- 2 tbsp fresh parsley, chopped
- Egg noodles or rice, to serve

**Instructions:**

1. Heat olive oil in a large skillet over medium-high heat.
2. Add beef slices and cook until browned. Remove beef and set aside.
3. In the same skillet, sauté onion and garlic until soft.
4. Sprinkle flour over the onions and garlic, stirring to combine.
5. Gradually add beef broth, Worcestershire sauce, and Dijon mustard, stirring until smooth.
6. Stir in sour cream and simmer for 5 minutes.
7. Return beef to the skillet, season with salt and pepper, and cook for another 2-3 minutes.
8. Serve over egg noodles or rice, and garnish with fresh parsley.

**Spaghetti Carbonara**

**Ingredients:**

- 12 oz spaghetti
- 4 oz pancetta or bacon, diced
- 3 large eggs
- 1 cup grated Parmesan cheese
- 2 cloves garlic, minced
- Salt and pepper, to taste
- Fresh parsley, chopped (optional)

**Instructions:**

1. Cook spaghetti according to package instructions.
2. In a separate pan, cook pancetta or bacon until crispy. Remove from pan.
3. In a bowl, whisk together eggs, Parmesan, salt, and pepper.
4. In the pan with pancetta drippings, sauté garlic until fragrant.
5. Add cooked spaghetti to the pan and toss to coat.
6. Remove from heat and quickly stir in egg mixture, allowing the heat to cook the eggs and create a creamy sauce.
7. Stir in pancetta or bacon and season with more salt and pepper.
8. Garnish with parsley, if desired, and serve immediately.

**Chicken Parmesan**

**Ingredients:**

- 4 boneless, skinless chicken breasts
- 1 cup all-purpose flour
- 2 eggs, beaten
- 1 cup breadcrumbs (preferably Italian-style)
- 1 cup marinara sauce
- 2 cups shredded mozzarella cheese
- 1/2 cup grated Parmesan cheese
- 2 tbsp olive oil
- Salt and pepper, to taste
- Fresh basil, for garnish

**Instructions:**

1. Preheat oven to 400°F (200°C).
2. Season chicken breasts with salt and pepper.
3. Dredge chicken in flour, dip in beaten eggs, and coat with breadcrumbs.
4. Heat olive oil in a skillet over medium heat and cook chicken for 3-4 minutes per side until golden.
5. Transfer chicken to a baking dish and top with marinara sauce, mozzarella, and Parmesan.
6. Bake for 20-25 minutes, until chicken reaches an internal temperature of 165°F and cheese is bubbly.
7. Garnish with fresh basil and serve.

## Homemade Mac and Cheese

### Ingredients:

- 8 oz elbow macaroni
- 2 cups shredded sharp cheddar cheese
- 1/2 cup grated Parmesan cheese
- 2 tbsp butter
- 2 tbsp flour
- 2 cups milk
- 1/2 tsp mustard powder
- Salt and pepper, to taste

### Instructions:

1. Cook macaroni according to package instructions, then drain and set aside.
2. In a saucepan, melt butter over medium heat.
3. Stir in flour and cook for 1-2 minutes to form a roux.
4. Gradually whisk in milk and cook until the sauce thickens.
5. Stir in cheddar and Parmesan cheese until melted and smooth.
6. Season with mustard powder, salt, and pepper.
7. Toss cooked macaroni in the cheese sauce until well-coated.
8. Serve warm.

**Classic Meatloaf**

**Ingredients:**

- 1 lb ground beef
- 1/2 lb ground pork
- 1 small onion, finely chopped
- 2 cloves garlic, minced
- 1/2 cup breadcrumbs
- 1/4 cup milk
- 1 large egg
- 1/4 cup ketchup
- 2 tbsp Worcestershire sauce
- 1 tsp dried thyme
- Salt and pepper, to taste
- 1/4 cup ketchup (for topping)

**Instructions:**

1. Preheat oven to 350°F (175°C).
2. In a large bowl, combine ground beef, ground pork, onion, garlic, breadcrumbs, milk, egg, ketchup, Worcestershire sauce, thyme, salt, and pepper.
3. Mix well and shape into a loaf.
4. Place in a greased baking dish and top with additional ketchup.
5. Bake for 1 hour, or until the meatloaf reaches an internal temperature of 160°F (71°C).
6. Let rest before slicing and serving.

**Garlic Butter Shrimp**

**Ingredients:**

- 1 lb large shrimp, peeled and deveined
- 4 tbsp butter
- 4 cloves garlic, minced
- 1 tbsp lemon juice
- Salt and pepper, to taste
- Fresh parsley, chopped, for garnish

**Instructions:**

1. Heat butter in a large skillet over medium heat.
2. Add garlic and cook for 1-2 minutes, until fragrant.
3. Add shrimp, season with salt and pepper, and cook for 2-3 minutes per side until pink and cooked through.
4. Stir in lemon juice and toss to coat.
5. Garnish with parsley and serve.

**Baked Ziti**

**Ingredients:**

- 1 lb ziti pasta
- 2 cups marinara sauce
- 1 lb ricotta cheese
- 2 cups shredded mozzarella cheese
- 1/2 cup grated Parmesan cheese
- 1 tbsp dried basil
- 1 tbsp dried oregano
- Salt and pepper, to taste

**Instructions:**

1. Preheat oven to 375°F (190°C).
2. Cook ziti pasta according to package instructions, then drain.
3. In a large bowl, mix cooked pasta, marinara sauce, ricotta cheese, mozzarella, Parmesan, basil, oregano, salt, and pepper.
4. Transfer to a greased baking dish and top with extra mozzarella.
5. Bake for 25-30 minutes, until the cheese is melted and bubbly.
6. Serve warm.

**Chicken Alfredo Pasta**

**Ingredients:**

- 2 chicken breasts, boneless and skinless
- 12 oz fettuccine pasta
- 2 tbsp olive oil
- 2 cloves garlic, minced
- 1 cup heavy cream
- 1 cup grated Parmesan cheese
- Salt and pepper, to taste
- Fresh parsley, chopped, for garnish

**Instructions:**

1. Cook fettuccine according to package instructions, then drain and set aside.
2. Season chicken breasts with salt and pepper.
3. Heat olive oil in a skillet over medium-high heat and cook chicken for 6-7 minutes per side until cooked through.
4. Remove chicken and slice.
5. In the same skillet, sauté garlic in butter until fragrant, then add heavy cream and bring to a simmer.
6. Stir in Parmesan cheese and cook until the sauce thickens.
7. Toss pasta with the Alfredo sauce and top with sliced chicken.
8. Garnish with parsley and serve.

**Slow Cooker Pot Roast**

**Ingredients:**

- 3-4 lb beef chuck roast
- 1 onion, quartered
- 4 carrots, cut into chunks
- 4 potatoes, cut into chunks
- 4 cloves garlic, minced
- 2 cups beef broth
- 1 tbsp Worcestershire sauce
- 1 tsp dried thyme
- Salt and pepper, to taste

**Instructions:**

1. Season the roast with salt, pepper, and thyme.
2. Place the roast in a slow cooker and surround it with vegetables.
3. Add garlic, beef broth, and Worcestershire sauce.
4. Cover and cook on low for 8 hours or until the meat is tender.
5. Serve with the vegetables and juices.

**Stuffed Bell Peppers**

**Ingredients:**

- 4 large bell peppers, tops cut off and seeds removed
- 1 lb ground beef or turkey
- 1 cup cooked rice
- 1 small onion, chopped
- 1 cup marinara sauce
- 1 cup shredded mozzarella cheese
- Salt and pepper, to taste

**Instructions:**

1. Preheat oven to 375°F (190°C).
2. In a skillet, cook the ground meat and onion until browned.
3. Stir in cooked rice and marinara sauce, and season with salt and pepper.
4. Stuff the peppers with the mixture and place in a baking dish.
5. Top with shredded mozzarella cheese.
6. Cover with foil and bake for 30 minutes, then uncover and bake for another 10 minutes until the cheese is melted.
7. Serve warm.

**Shepherd's Pie**

**Ingredients:**

- 1 lb ground beef or lamb
- 1 small onion, chopped
- 2 cloves garlic, minced
- 1 cup frozen peas and carrots
- 2 cups mashed potatoes
- 1 cup beef broth
- 1 tbsp Worcestershire sauce
- Salt and pepper, to taste

**Instructions:**

1. Preheat oven to 400°F (200°C).
2. In a skillet, cook the ground meat, onion, and garlic until browned.
3. Add peas and carrots, Worcestershire sauce, beef broth, salt, and pepper.
4. Simmer for 5 minutes, then transfer to a baking dish.
5. Spread mashed potatoes over the top.
6. Bake for 20 minutes, until the top is golden brown.
7. Serve warm.

**Chicken Tikka Masala**

**Ingredients:**

- 1 lb chicken breast or thighs, cubed
- 1 tbsp garam masala
- 1 tsp cumin
- 1 tsp turmeric
- 1 tsp coriander
- 2 tbsp plain yogurt
- 2 tbsp vegetable oil
- 1 onion, chopped
- 2 cloves garlic, minced
- 1 tbsp grated ginger
- 1 can (14 oz) diced tomatoes
- 1 cup heavy cream
- Salt and pepper, to taste

**Instructions:**

1. Marinate chicken with yogurt, garam masala, cumin, turmeric, coriander, salt, and pepper for at least 30 minutes.
2. Heat oil in a skillet, sauté onion, garlic, and ginger until soft.
3. Add marinated chicken and cook until browned.
4. Add tomatoes and simmer for 10 minutes.
5. Stir in heavy cream and cook for another 5 minutes.
6. Serve with rice or naan.

## French Onion Soup

### Ingredients:

- 4 large onions, thinly sliced
- 4 cups beef broth
- 1/2 cup white wine
- 2 tbsp butter
- 1 tsp sugar
- 2 cloves garlic, minced
- 1 tbsp fresh thyme
- Salt and pepper, to taste
- 4 slices French bread, toasted
- 1 cup grated Gruyère cheese

### Instructions:

1. In a large pot, melt butter and sauté onions with sugar until caramelized, about 25 minutes.
2. Add garlic, thyme, salt, and pepper, and cook for 1 more minute.
3. Pour in wine and broth, and simmer for 15 minutes.
4. Ladle soup into bowls, top with toast, and sprinkle with Gruyère.
5. Broil for 2-3 minutes until cheese is melted and bubbly.
6. Serve warm.

## BBQ Pulled Pork

### Ingredients:

- 3-4 lb pork shoulder
- 1 cup BBQ sauce
- 1/2 cup apple cider vinegar
- 1 tbsp brown sugar
- 1 tbsp smoked paprika
- 1 tbsp garlic powder
- 1 tbsp onion powder
- Salt and pepper, to taste

### Instructions:

1. Season pork with paprika, garlic powder, onion powder, salt, and pepper.
2. Place in a slow cooker and add BBQ sauce, apple cider vinegar, and brown sugar.
3. Cover and cook on low for 8 hours, until the pork is tender.
4. Shred the pork with two forks and mix with the sauce.
5. Serve on buns or with sides.

**Shrimp Scampi**

**Ingredients:**

- 1 lb large shrimp, peeled and deveined
- 8 oz spaghetti or linguine
- 4 tbsp butter
- 3 cloves garlic, minced
- 1/2 cup white wine
- 1 tbsp lemon juice
- 1/2 tsp red pepper flakes (optional)
- Salt and pepper, to taste
- Fresh parsley, chopped, for garnish

**Instructions:**

1. Cook pasta according to package instructions, then drain and set aside.
2. In a large skillet, melt butter over medium heat.
3. Add garlic and red pepper flakes (if using), and cook for 1-2 minutes.
4. Add shrimp, season with salt and pepper, and cook until pink, about 3-4 minutes.
5. Pour in white wine and lemon juice, simmer for 2 minutes.
6. Toss in cooked pasta and coat with sauce.
7. Garnish with fresh parsley and serve immediately.

## Homemade Pizza

**Ingredients:**

- 1 lb pizza dough (store-bought or homemade)
- 1/2 cup tomato sauce
- 2 cups shredded mozzarella cheese
- Toppings of your choice (pepperoni, bell peppers, onions, mushrooms, olives, etc.)
- Olive oil, for brushing

**Instructions:**

1. Preheat oven to 475°F (245°C).
2. Roll out the pizza dough on a floured surface to your desired thickness.
3. Transfer the dough to a greased baking sheet or pizza stone.
4. Spread tomato sauce evenly over the dough.
5. Sprinkle with mozzarella cheese and add your favorite toppings.
6. Brush the edges of the dough with olive oil for a golden finish.
7. Bake for 10-12 minutes, until the crust is golden and cheese is bubbly.
8. Slice and serve.

**Chicken Fajitas**

**Ingredients:**

- 1 lb boneless, skinless chicken breasts, sliced
- 1 bell pepper, sliced
- 1 onion, sliced
- 2 tbsp olive oil
- 1 tbsp chili powder
- 1 tsp cumin
- 1 tsp paprika
- 1/2 tsp garlic powder
- Salt and pepper, to taste
- 8 flour tortillas
- Lime wedges, for serving
- Fresh cilantro, for garnish

**Instructions:**

1. In a bowl, mix olive oil, chili powder, cumin, paprika, garlic powder, salt, and pepper.
2. Toss chicken in the spice mixture to coat evenly.
3. Heat a skillet over medium-high heat, and cook chicken until browned and cooked through, about 5-7 minutes.
4. Add bell pepper and onion to the skillet, cooking until softened, about 3-4 minutes.
5. Warm tortillas in a dry skillet or microwave.
6. Serve chicken and vegetables in tortillas, garnished with lime wedges and fresh cilantro.

**Baked Salmon with Lemon**

**Ingredients:**

- 4 salmon fillets
- 2 tbsp olive oil
- 1 lemon, thinly sliced
- 2 cloves garlic, minced
- 1 tbsp fresh dill or parsley, chopped
- Salt and pepper, to taste

**Instructions:**

1. Preheat oven to 400°F (200°C).
2. Place salmon fillets on a lined baking sheet.
3. Drizzle with olive oil and sprinkle with salt, pepper, and minced garlic.
4. Top with lemon slices and fresh dill or parsley.
5. Bake for 12-15 minutes, until the salmon flakes easily with a fork.
6. Serve warm with your favorite sides.

**Creamy Mushroom Risotto**

**Ingredients:**

- 1 cup Arborio rice
- 2 tbsp butter
- 1 small onion, chopped
- 2 cups mushrooms, sliced
- 1/2 cup white wine
- 4 cups chicken or vegetable broth, warmed
- 1/2 cup grated Parmesan cheese
- Salt and pepper, to taste
- Fresh parsley, chopped, for garnish

**Instructions:**

1. In a large pan, melt butter over medium heat.
2. Add onion and cook until soft, about 3 minutes.
3. Add mushrooms and cook until tender, about 5 minutes.
4. Stir in Arborio rice and cook for 1-2 minutes.
5. Pour in white wine and stir until absorbed.
6. Gradually add warm broth, 1/2 cup at a time, stirring constantly until the liquid is absorbed before adding more.
7. Once the rice is creamy and tender (about 20-25 minutes), stir in Parmesan cheese and season with salt and pepper.
8. Garnish with fresh parsley and serve.

**Classic Lasagna**

**Ingredients:**

- 12 lasagna noodles, cooked
- 1 lb ground beef or pork
- 1 onion, chopped
- 2 cloves garlic, minced
- 1 jar (24 oz) marinara sauce
- 1 1/2 cups ricotta cheese
- 2 cups shredded mozzarella cheese
- 1/2 cup grated Parmesan cheese
- 1 egg
- 1 tbsp dried basil
- 1 tsp dried oregano
- Salt and pepper, to taste

**Instructions:**

1. Preheat oven to 375°F (190°C).
2. In a skillet, cook ground meat, onion, and garlic until browned.
3. Add marinara sauce, basil, oregano, salt, and pepper. Simmer for 10 minutes.
4. In a bowl, mix ricotta cheese, egg, Parmesan cheese, and a pinch of salt.
5. In a baking dish, spread a layer of meat sauce, followed by lasagna noodles, ricotta mixture, and mozzarella. Repeat layers.
6. Top with remaining meat sauce and mozzarella.
7. Cover with foil and bake for 30 minutes. Uncover and bake for another 10-15 minutes, until cheese is bubbly.
8. Let rest before slicing and serving.

**Beef Tacos**

**Ingredients:**

- 1 lb ground beef
- 1 small onion, chopped
- 1 packet taco seasoning
- 1/2 cup water
- 8 taco shells or tortillas
- Toppings: shredded lettuce, cheese, salsa, sour cream, avocado

**Instructions:**

1. In a skillet, cook ground beef and onion until browned.
2. Stir in taco seasoning and water, simmer for 5 minutes.
3. Warm taco shells in the oven or microwave.
4. Fill taco shells with beef mixture and top with desired toppings.
5. Serve immediately.

## Lemon Herb Roast Chicken

### Ingredients:

- 1 whole chicken (about 4-5 lbs)
- 2 tbsp olive oil
- 1 lemon, quartered
- 4 garlic cloves, smashed
- 1 tbsp fresh thyme or rosemary
- Salt and pepper, to taste

### Instructions:

1. Preheat oven to 425°F (220°C).
2. Pat chicken dry and rub with olive oil.
3. Stuff the cavity with lemon quarters, garlic, and fresh herbs.
4. Season the chicken with salt and pepper.
5. Roast for 1 hour 15 minutes, or until the internal temperature reaches 165°F (75°C).
6. Let rest before carving and serving.

**Clam Chowder**

**Ingredients:**

- 2 cans (6.5 oz) chopped clams
- 4 slices bacon, chopped
- 1 small onion, chopped
- 2 celery stalks, chopped
- 2 cloves garlic, minced
- 2 cups potatoes, peeled and diced
- 1 1/2 cups heavy cream
- 2 cups chicken broth
- 1 tsp dried thyme
- Salt and pepper, to taste
- Fresh parsley, for garnish

**Instructions:**

1. In a large pot, cook bacon until crispy, then remove and set aside.
2. Add onion, celery, and garlic to the bacon drippings and cook until soft.
3. Add potatoes, chicken broth, thyme, salt, and pepper. Bring to a boil, then simmer for 10-15 minutes until potatoes are tender.
4. Stir in clams (with juice) and heavy cream.
5. Simmer for 5-7 minutes, then garnish with crispy bacon and fresh parsley.
6. Serve warm with crusty bread.

**Crispy Fried Chicken**

**Ingredients:**

- 4 chicken pieces (drumsticks or thighs)
- 2 cups buttermilk
- 2 cups all-purpose flour
- 1 tbsp paprika
- 1 tbsp garlic powder
- 1 tbsp onion powder
- 1 tsp salt
- 1 tsp black pepper
- 1/2 tsp cayenne pepper (optional)
- Vegetable oil, for frying

**Instructions:**

1. Marinate the chicken in buttermilk for at least 2 hours or overnight.
2. In a shallow bowl, mix flour, paprika, garlic powder, onion powder, salt, pepper, and cayenne.
3. Heat oil in a large skillet over medium-high heat (about 350°F).
4. Dredge the chicken in the seasoned flour, pressing down to coat well.
5. Fry chicken in batches for 10-15 minutes, turning occasionally until golden brown and the internal temperature reaches 165°F (75°C).
6. Drain on paper towels and serve hot.

**Teriyaki Chicken**

**Ingredients:**

- 4 boneless, skinless chicken breasts
- 1/2 cup soy sauce
- 1/4 cup honey
- 2 tbsp rice vinegar
- 2 tbsp sesame oil
- 2 cloves garlic, minced
- 1 tbsp grated ginger
- 1 tbsp cornstarch (optional for thickening)
- Sesame seeds and green onions for garnish

**Instructions:**

1. In a bowl, whisk together soy sauce, honey, rice vinegar, sesame oil, garlic, and ginger.
2. Marinate the chicken in the sauce for at least 30 minutes.
3. Heat a skillet over medium heat and cook the chicken for 5-7 minutes per side, until fully cooked.
4. If you want a thicker sauce, mix cornstarch with a little water and stir into the sauce, simmering for a few minutes.
5. Serve the chicken with the sauce, garnished with sesame seeds and green onions.

**Chicken and Dumplings**

**Ingredients:**

- 1 lb chicken breast or thighs, cooked and shredded
- 1 medium onion, chopped
- 2 carrots, sliced
- 2 celery stalks, chopped
- 4 cups chicken broth
- 1 cup milk
- 2 cups flour
- 1/2 tsp baking powder
- 1/4 tsp salt
- 1/4 tsp pepper
- 2 tbsp butter
- 1/4 cup chopped parsley

**Instructions:**

1. In a large pot, melt butter and sauté onions, carrots, and celery until soft, about 5 minutes.
2. Add chicken broth, milk, and shredded chicken. Bring to a simmer.
3. In a bowl, combine flour, baking powder, salt, and pepper. Add milk until a thick batter forms.
4. Drop spoonfuls of the dough into the simmering soup.
5. Cover and cook for 15-20 minutes until the dumplings are cooked through.
6. Garnish with parsley and serve.

**Sweet and Sour Pork**

**Ingredients:**

- 1 lb pork tenderloin, cubed
- 1/2 cup flour
- 1/2 tsp salt
- 1/2 tsp pepper
- 1 egg, beaten
- 1/2 cup vegetable oil, for frying
- 1 bell pepper, chopped
- 1 onion, chopped
- 1/2 cup pineapple chunks
- 1/2 cup ketchup
- 1/4 cup rice vinegar
- 1/4 cup brown sugar
- 1 tbsp soy sauce
- 1 tbsp cornstarch mixed with 2 tbsp water (for thickening)

**Instructions:**

1. Toss pork cubes in flour, salt, and pepper, then dip in egg.
2. Heat oil in a skillet and fry pork in batches until golden brown. Drain on paper towels.
3. In the same skillet, sauté bell pepper, onion, and pineapple until softened.
4. In a bowl, whisk together ketchup, vinegar, brown sugar, soy sauce, and cornstarch mixture.
5. Add sauce to the vegetables and simmer for 2-3 minutes until thickened.
6. Return pork to the skillet and toss to coat in sauce. Serve hot.

## Homemade Chili

### Ingredients:

- 1 lb ground beef or turkey
- 1 onion, chopped
- 2 cloves garlic, minced
- 2 cans (15 oz) kidney beans, drained
- 1 can (15 oz) diced tomatoes
- 1 can (6 oz) tomato paste
- 1 tbsp chili powder
- 1 tsp cumin
- 1/2 tsp paprika
- Salt and pepper, to taste
- 1 cup beef broth

### Instructions:

1. In a large pot, brown the ground meat with onions and garlic.
2. Add beans, tomatoes, tomato paste, chili powder, cumin, paprika, salt, pepper, and beef broth.
3. Simmer for 30-40 minutes, stirring occasionally.
4. Adjust seasoning and serve hot with toppings like cheese, sour cream, and green onions.

**Chicken Pot Pie**

**Ingredients:**

- 2 cups cooked chicken, shredded
- 1 cup frozen peas and carrots
- 1/2 cup celery, chopped
- 1/2 cup onion, chopped
- 1 cup chicken broth
- 1 cup milk
- 1/4 cup flour
- 1/4 tsp thyme
- Salt and pepper, to taste
- 1 sheet pie crust, thawed

**Instructions:**

1. Preheat oven to 375°F (190°C).
2. In a skillet, cook onion and celery until softened. Add peas, carrots, and chicken.
3. Stir in flour and cook for 1-2 minutes. Gradually add chicken broth and milk, stirring until thickened.
4. Season with thyme, salt, and pepper.
5. Pour the mixture into a pie dish and cover with pie crust.
6. Bake for 25-30 minutes, until golden brown. Let cool for a few minutes before serving.

**Beef and Broccoli Stir-Fry**

**Ingredients:**

- 1 lb beef sirloin, thinly sliced
- 2 cups broccoli florets
- 1/4 cup soy sauce
- 1 tbsp oyster sauce
- 1 tbsp sesame oil
- 2 cloves garlic, minced
- 1 tsp ginger, grated
- 2 tbsp vegetable oil for stir-frying

**Instructions:**

1. In a bowl, mix soy sauce, oyster sauce, sesame oil, garlic, and ginger.
2. Heat vegetable oil in a wok or skillet over medium-high heat.
3. Add beef and stir-fry for 2-3 minutes until browned.
4. Add broccoli and stir-fry for another 3-4 minutes until tender-crisp.
5. Pour sauce over beef and broccoli, toss to coat, and cook for another minute.
6. Serve hot with rice.

**Grilled Cheese and Tomato Soup**

**Ingredients (Grilled Cheese):**

- 8 slices bread
- 4 slices cheddar cheese
- 4 tbsp butter

**Ingredients (Tomato Soup):**

- 1 can (28 oz) crushed tomatoes
- 1 onion, chopped
- 2 cloves garlic, minced
- 1 cup vegetable broth
- 1 tsp sugar
- Salt and pepper, to taste
- 1/2 cup heavy cream (optional)

**Instructions (Grilled Cheese):**

1. Butter each slice of bread and place cheese in between.
2. Heat a skillet over medium heat and grill the sandwiches until golden brown and cheese is melted, about 3-4 minutes per side.

**Instructions (Tomato Soup):**

1. In a pot, sauté onion and garlic until softened.
2. Add crushed tomatoes, vegetable broth, and sugar. Simmer for 15-20 minutes.
3. Blend until smooth (optional) and stir in heavy cream.
4. Season with salt and pepper. Serve with grilled cheese.

**Tuna Casserole**

**Ingredients:**

- 2 cans (5 oz) tuna, drained
- 8 oz egg noodles, cooked
- 1 can (10.5 oz) cream of mushroom soup
- 1/2 cup frozen peas
- 1/2 cup grated cheddar cheese
- 1/2 cup breadcrumbs
- 1 tbsp butter

**Instructions:**

1. Preheat oven to 375°F (190°C).
2. In a large bowl, mix tuna, cooked noodles, cream of mushroom soup, peas, and cheese.
3. Pour into a greased baking dish and top with breadcrumbs and butter.
4. Bake for 20-25 minutes, until bubbly and golden brown.

**Meatball Subs**

**Ingredients:**

- 12 meatballs (store-bought or homemade)
- 1 jar marinara sauce
- 4 sub rolls
- 1 cup shredded mozzarella cheese

**Instructions:**

1. Heat meatballs and marinara sauce in a pot over medium heat for 10-15 minutes.
2. Slice sub rolls and place meatballs inside.
3. Top with marinara sauce and shredded mozzarella.
4. Bake at 375°F (190°C) for 5-7 minutes, until the cheese is melted.
5. Serve hot.

**Pancakes from Scratch**

**Ingredients:**

- 1 1/2 cups all-purpose flour
- 3 1/2 tsp baking powder
- 1 tbsp sugar
- 1/2 tsp salt
- 1 1/4 cups milk
- 1 egg
- 3 tbsp butter, melted
- 1 tsp vanilla extract

**Instructions:**

1. In a large bowl, whisk together flour, baking powder, sugar, and salt.
2. In a separate bowl, whisk together milk, egg, melted butter, and vanilla.
3. Pour wet ingredients into dry ingredients and stir until just combined.
4. Heat a griddle or skillet over medium heat and lightly grease it.
5. Pour 1/4 cup of batter onto the griddle and cook until bubbles form on the surface, then flip and cook until golden brown on both sides.
6. Serve with syrup and toppings of your choice.

**French Toast**

**Ingredients:**

- 4 slices of bread (preferably day-old)
- 2 eggs
- 1/2 cup milk
- 1/2 tsp cinnamon
- 1/2 tsp vanilla extract
- 1 tbsp butter
- Powdered sugar and syrup, for serving

**Instructions:**

1. In a bowl, whisk together eggs, milk, cinnamon, and vanilla.
2. Heat a skillet over medium heat and melt butter.
3. Dip bread slices into the egg mixture, ensuring both sides are coated.
4. Cook the bread on the skillet for 2-3 minutes per side, until golden brown.
5. Serve with powdered sugar and syrup.

**Shrimp Fried Rice**

**Ingredients:**

- 1 lb shrimp, peeled and deveined
- 3 cups cooked rice (preferably cold)
- 2 tbsp soy sauce
- 1 tbsp sesame oil
- 1/2 onion, chopped
- 2 cloves garlic, minced
- 1/2 cup frozen peas and carrots
- 2 eggs, beaten
- Green onions, chopped, for garnish

**Instructions:**

1. Heat sesame oil in a large skillet or wok over medium-high heat.
2. Add shrimp and cook until pink, about 3-4 minutes. Remove shrimp and set aside.
3. In the same skillet, add onions and garlic, cooking until softened.
4. Add peas and carrots, and cook for another 2 minutes.
5. Push the vegetables to the side and scramble the eggs in the skillet.
6. Add cold rice to the skillet, along with soy sauce, and stir to combine.
7. Add shrimp back in and toss everything together.
8. Garnish with green onions and serve.

**Classic Caesar Salad with Chicken**

**Ingredients:**

- 2 chicken breasts, grilled and sliced
- 4 cups Romaine lettuce, chopped
- 1/2 cup Caesar dressing
- 1/4 cup grated Parmesan cheese
- Croutons, for topping

**Instructions:**

1. Grill or pan-sear the chicken breasts until fully cooked, then slice thinly.
2. In a large bowl, toss chopped lettuce with Caesar dressing.
3. Top with sliced chicken, Parmesan cheese, and croutons.
4. Serve immediately.

**Homemade Burgers**

**Ingredients:**

- 1 lb ground beef (80% lean)
- 1/4 cup breadcrumbs
- 1 egg
- 1 tbsp Worcestershire sauce
- 1 tsp garlic powder
- Salt and pepper, to taste
- Burger buns
- Toppings: lettuce, tomato, cheese, pickles, etc.

**Instructions:**

1. In a bowl, mix ground beef, breadcrumbs, egg, Worcestershire sauce, garlic powder, salt, and pepper.
2. Shape the mixture into 4 equal patties.
3. Heat a grill or skillet over medium-high heat and cook patties for 4-5 minutes per side, or until desired doneness.
4. Toast burger buns on the grill or in a skillet.
5. Assemble burgers with your favorite toppings and serve.

**Beef Wellington**

**Ingredients:**

- 2 lb beef tenderloin
- Salt and pepper, to taste
- 2 tbsp olive oil
- 1/2 cup Dijon mustard
- 1/2 lb mushrooms, finely chopped
- 2 tbsp butter
- 1/4 cup brandy or white wine
- 1 package puff pastry
- 1 egg, beaten

**Instructions:**

1. Preheat oven to 400°F (200°C).
2. Season the beef tenderloin with salt and pepper. Sear it in olive oil over high heat for 2-3 minutes on each side, then brush with Dijon mustard.
3. In a pan, melt butter and sauté mushrooms until the moisture evaporates and the mixture becomes dry. Add brandy or wine and cook until evaporated.
4. Roll out the puff pastry on a floured surface. Spread the mushroom mixture over the pastry and place the beef on top. Wrap the beef tightly in the pastry.
5. Brush the pastry with beaten egg and bake for 30-40 minutes, until golden brown.
6. Let it rest for 10 minutes before slicing and serving.

**Cajun Jambalaya**

**Ingredients:**

- 1 lb chicken breast, diced
- 1/2 lb andouille sausage, sliced
- 1 onion, chopped
- 1 bell pepper, chopped
- 2 celery stalks, chopped
- 2 cloves garlic, minced
- 1 can (14.5 oz) diced tomatoes
- 1 1/2 cups rice
- 3 cups chicken broth
- 1 tsp paprika
- 1/2 tsp cayenne pepper
- Salt and pepper, to taste
- 1/2 tsp thyme
- 2 tbsp parsley, chopped

**Instructions:**

1. In a large pot, sauté chicken and sausage over medium heat until browned.
2. Add onion, bell pepper, celery, and garlic, and cook until softened.
3. Stir in tomatoes, rice, chicken broth, paprika, cayenne, salt, pepper, and thyme.
4. Bring to a boil, then reduce heat and cover. Simmer for 20-25 minutes until the rice is cooked.
5. Garnish with parsley and serve.

## Greek Moussaka

### Ingredients:

- 1 lb ground lamb or beef
- 1 onion, chopped
- 2 cloves garlic, minced
- 2 cups tomato sauce
- 1 tsp cinnamon
- 1/4 tsp nutmeg
- 2 eggplants, sliced
- 1 cup béchamel sauce (butter, flour, milk, and Parmesan)
- 1/4 cup grated Parmesan cheese

### Instructions:

1. Preheat oven to 375°F (190°C).
2. Sauté ground meat with onion and garlic until browned, then add tomato sauce, cinnamon, and nutmeg. Simmer for 20 minutes.
3. Slice eggplants and grill or roast them until tender.
4. In a baking dish, layer eggplants, followed by meat sauce, and top with béchamel sauce.
5. Repeat layers and finish with béchamel sauce.
6. Sprinkle with Parmesan and bake for 30 minutes until golden and bubbly.
7. Let it cool for 10 minutes before serving.

**Korean Bibimbap**

**Ingredients:**

- 2 cups cooked rice
- 1/2 lb ground beef or chicken
- 1/2 cup spinach, sautéed
- 1/2 cup carrots, julienned
- 1/2 cup cucumber, julienned
- 1/4 cup kimchi (optional)
- 2 eggs (fried sunny-side-up)
- 2 tbsp sesame oil
- 2 tbsp gochujang (Korean chili paste)
- Sesame seeds, for garnish

**Instructions:**

1. In a skillet, cook ground meat with sesame oil until browned.
2. Prepare vegetables by sautéing spinach and julienning carrots and cucumbers.
3. In bowls, place rice and top with meat, spinach, carrots, cucumber, kimchi, and a fried egg.
4. Drizzle with gochujang and sprinkle with sesame seeds.
5. Mix everything together before eating.

**Vegetable Stir-Fry**

**Ingredients:**

- 1 cup broccoli florets
- 1 bell pepper, sliced
- 1 carrot, sliced
- 1/2 onion, sliced
- 1 zucchini, sliced
- 2 tbsp soy sauce
- 1 tbsp sesame oil
- 1 tbsp rice vinegar
- 1 tbsp honey
- 2 cloves garlic, minced
- Cooked rice, for serving

**Instructions:**

1. Heat sesame oil in a large skillet or wok over medium-high heat.
2. Add garlic and cook until fragrant, about 1 minute.
3. Add vegetables and stir-fry for 5-7 minutes, until tender-crisp.
4. Mix in soy sauce, rice vinegar, and honey, and cook for another 2-3 minutes.
5. Serve over cooked rice.

## Slow Cooker Ribs

### Ingredients:

- 2 racks of baby back ribs
- 1 cup barbecue sauce
- 2 tbsp brown sugar
- 1 tbsp paprika
- 1 tbsp garlic powder
- 1 tbsp onion powder
- 1 tsp salt
- 1 tsp black pepper
- 1 tsp smoked paprika (optional)

### Instructions:

1. Preheat the slow cooker.
2. Remove the silver skin from the ribs and rub both sides with the dry rub (brown sugar, paprika, garlic powder, onion powder, salt, pepper, and smoked paprika).
3. Place the ribs in the slow cooker and cover with barbecue sauce.
4. Cook on low for 6-8 hours or high for 3-4 hours until tender.
5. Optional: After slow cooking, broil the ribs in the oven for 3-5 minutes to get a crispy exterior.
6. Slice and serve with extra barbecue sauce.

**Lobster Bisque**

**Ingredients:**

- 2 lobsters (or 1 lb lobster meat)
- 4 tbsp butter
- 1 small onion, chopped
- 2 cloves garlic, minced
- 1/4 cup all-purpose flour
- 1 1/2 cups chicken broth
- 2 cups heavy cream
- 1/4 cup brandy (optional)
- 1 tbsp tomato paste
- 1 tsp paprika
- Salt and pepper to taste
- Fresh parsley for garnish

**Instructions:**

1. Boil the lobsters in salted water for about 8-10 minutes. Remove, let cool, and remove the meat from the shells. Set meat aside and reserve the shells.
2. In a pot, melt butter and sauté onions and garlic until softened.
3. Add flour and cook for 1-2 minutes to create a roux.
4. Slowly whisk in chicken broth and bring to a simmer.
5. Add the lobster shells and simmer for 20-30 minutes to infuse the broth.
6. Strain the broth and discard the shells.
7. Stir in heavy cream, brandy (optional), tomato paste, paprika, salt, and pepper.
8. Add the lobster meat and simmer for another 5-7 minutes.
9. Blend the soup until smooth using an immersion blender, then garnish with parsley before serving.

**Chicken Cordon Bleu**

**Ingredients:**

- 4 boneless, skinless chicken breasts
- 4 slices ham
- 4 slices Swiss cheese
- 1 cup breadcrumbs
- 1/2 cup flour
- 2 eggs, beaten
- 1 tbsp Dijon mustard
- 1 tbsp olive oil
- Salt and pepper, to taste
- 1/2 cup white wine (optional)

**Instructions:**

1. Preheat the oven to 375°F (190°C).
2. Pound the chicken breasts to an even thickness.
3. Place a slice of ham and a slice of cheese on each chicken breast, then roll them up and secure with toothpicks.
4. Dredge the chicken rolls in flour, then dip in beaten eggs, and coat with breadcrumbs.
5. Heat olive oil in a pan over medium-high heat and brown the chicken rolls on all sides (about 4 minutes per side).
6. Transfer the chicken to a baking dish and bake for 20-25 minutes until the chicken is cooked through.
7. Optionally, deglaze the pan with white wine and pour the sauce over the chicken before serving.

**Eggplant Parmesan**

**Ingredients:**

- 2 medium eggplants, sliced into 1/4-inch rounds
- 2 cups marinara sauce
- 2 cups shredded mozzarella cheese
- 1/2 cup grated Parmesan cheese
- 2 cups breadcrumbs
- 1/2 cup flour
- 2 eggs, beaten
- Olive oil, for frying
- Salt and pepper, to taste
- Fresh basil for garnish

**Instructions:**

1. Preheat oven to 375°F (190°C).
2. Dredge eggplant slices in flour, dip in beaten eggs, and coat with breadcrumbs.
3. Heat olive oil in a pan and fry eggplant slices until golden brown on both sides, about 2-3 minutes per side.
4. Layer the fried eggplant in a baking dish, covering with marinara sauce, mozzarella, and Parmesan.
5. Repeat the layers, finishing with cheese on top.
6. Bake for 20-25 minutes, until the cheese is bubbly and golden.
7. Garnish with fresh basil and serve.

**Classic Beef Stew**

**Ingredients:**

- 2 lbs beef stew meat, cubed
- 4 carrots, sliced
- 3 potatoes, peeled and diced
- 1 onion, chopped
- 3 cloves garlic, minced
- 4 cups beef broth
- 1 cup red wine (optional)
- 2 tbsp tomato paste
- 2 tsp dried thyme
- 1 tsp rosemary
- Salt and pepper to taste
- 2 tbsp flour (for thickening)

**Instructions:**

1. In a large pot, brown the beef stew meat in batches over medium-high heat. Remove and set aside.
2. Add onions and garlic to the pot and sauté until softened.
3. Stir in tomato paste and cook for 1-2 minutes.
4. Return the beef to the pot and add beef broth, red wine (if using), thyme, rosemary, salt, and pepper.
5. Bring to a simmer and cook for 1-1.5 hours, until the beef is tender.
6. Add carrots and potatoes and continue cooking for another 30 minutes, until the vegetables are tender.
7. If you want a thicker stew, mix flour with a little water and stir into the stew. Let it cook for 5 more minutes to thicken.
8. Serve hot.

**Apple Pie**

**Ingredients:**

- 6-8 medium apples (Granny Smith or Honeycrisp), peeled and sliced
- 1/2 cup granulated sugar
- 1/4 cup brown sugar
- 2 tbsp all-purpose flour
- 1 tsp cinnamon
- 1/4 tsp nutmeg
- 1 tbsp lemon juice
- 1 tbsp butter, cut into small pieces
- 1 package pie crusts (or homemade)
- 1 egg (for egg wash)

**Instructions:**

1. Preheat oven to 425°F (220°C).
2. In a large bowl, toss the apples with granulated sugar, brown sugar, flour, cinnamon, nutmeg, and lemon juice.
3. Roll out one pie crust and fit it into a pie dish.
4. Fill with the apple mixture and dot with butter.
5. Roll out the second pie crust and place it on top, sealing the edges.
6. Cut slits in the top of the pie to allow steam to escape.
7. Brush the top with a beaten egg for a golden crust.
8. Bake for 40-45 minutes, until the crust is golden and the filling is bubbling.
9. Let cool before serving.